The Chinese Zodiac

Lisa James

Contents

The Zodiac

There is a special Chinese **calendar.**
The calendar names each year after an animal.
These animals are part of the Chinese zodiac.

All of the animals are different.
Chinese **tradition** says that people born in the year of an animal are a bit like that animal too!

Let's see what the zodiac says about you.

Find the animal for the year you were born.

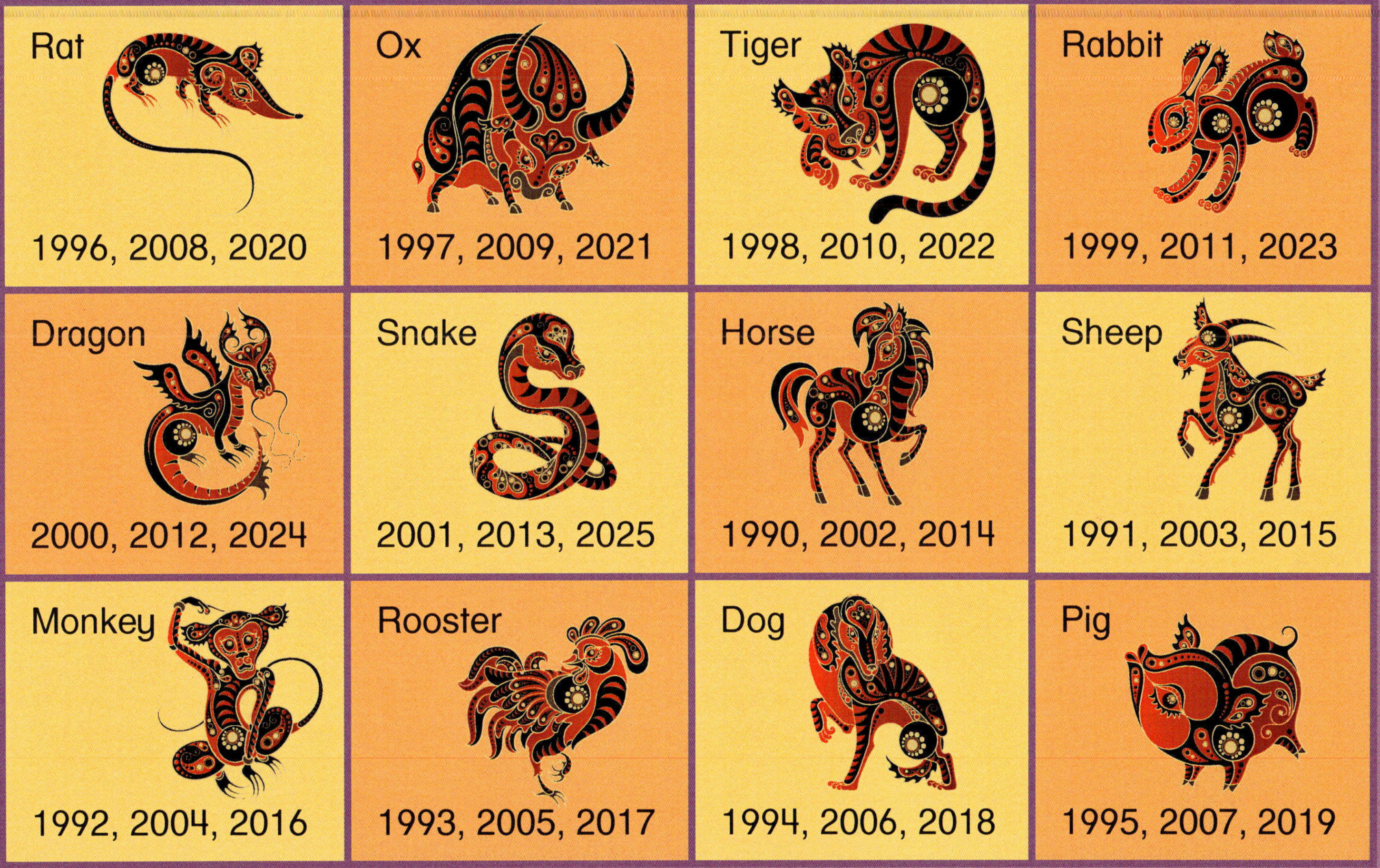

Rat

Rats are good at working out problems. They live in most parts of the world. They eat almost anything!

The zodiac says ...

People born in the year of the rat are smart.

Ox

An ox is a type of cow. **Oxen** are very strong and can pull big loads.

The zodiac says ...

People born in the year of the ox are hard workers.

Tiger

Tigers are strong and fast.
Tigers hunt for food.
They creep up on other animals!

The zodiac says ...

People born in the year of the tiger are brave.

Rabbit

Rabbits live in groups.
They have very long ears.
They like to eat grass!

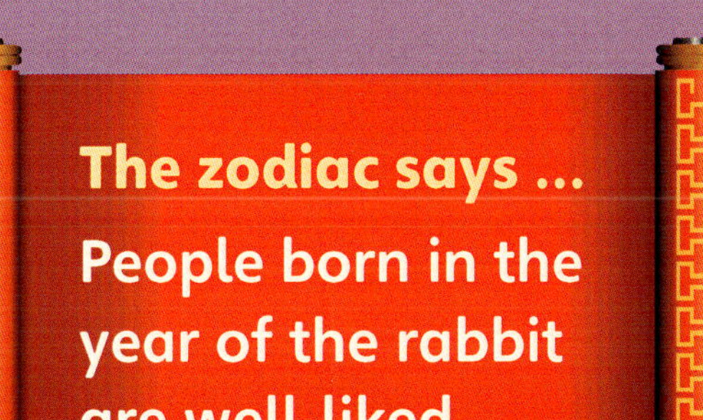

Dragon

A dragon is not a real animal.
Chinese stories say dragons are strong.

The zodiac says ...
People born in the year of the dragon are lucky.

Snake

Snakes like to lie in the sun to keep warm. They flick out their tongue to "smell" the air.

The zodiac says ...

People born in the year of the snake are mysterious.

Horse

Horses are friendly and smart.
They don't need much sleep.
They can even sleep standing up!

The zodiac says ...

People born in the year of the horse have lots of energy.

Sheep

Sheep keep close together to stay safe. Wild sheep have long, curving horns.

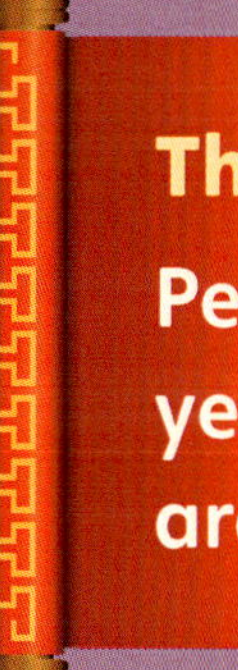

The zodiac says ...

People born in the year of the sheep are friendly.

Monkey

Monkeys are very clever.
They like to play.
They like to **groom** each other, too.

The zodiac says ...

People born in the year of the monkey are happy.

Rooster

Roosters crow loudly – “cock-a-doodle-doo”. They have a red comb on top of their head.

The zodiac says ...

People born in the year of the rooster are **practical.**

Dog

Dogs have a very good sense of smell. Many people have dogs as pets.

The zodiac says ...

People born in the year of the dog are **loyal**.

Pig

Pigs are very smart.
They roll in the mud to keep cool.
They use their snout to help them find food.

The zodiac says ...

People born in the year of the pig are kind.

Glossary

calendar a system used to measure time

groom clean

loyal faithful; not changing your belief in someone or something

oxen plural of ox

practical good at doing useful things

traditional handed down from age to age; relating to customs